How to become an honest con artist

Manuel Vera López

Revision by Jenifer Anne Queen
Illustration by Raúl Gómez Salvador

ISBN: **1502849666**
ISBN9-13 **9781502849663**

DEDICATION

To my father. We will get through these dark hours, and we will be well prepared for better days.

CONTENTS

SPECIAL THANKS

Special thanks to Jenifer Anne Queen for the massive task of reviewing this book and for her patience. And to Raúl Gómez Salvador who has been able to draw the idea I had in my mind for the cover.

1 INTRODUCTION

Who are you? That is not a metaphysical question. It's an open, direct and simple (rude also) question. It sounds bad, doesn't it?

But the truth is this is the question that everyone will ask themselves about you. And you will ask the same question about others: Who wrote this? Says who? What has he done so that I should trust him? Why is he an expert? Why should I agree with him? Who is he?

The world has changed. Our life is online now. We meet people, buy, have fun, search, investigate, train, talk, write, watch films, read books, look for a job, load pictures with friends, tag them or we change our personal status to "it's complicated".

Do we realize what are we doing? Do we notice the enormous amount of information we are giving away so others can find it?

Some say it's dangerous; it's the "big brother, "and we shall regret the loss of privacy. But where some see a problem, others see an opportunity.

Look at it from a professional point of view: in this new reality, if you know how to handle it, you can sell yourself! Social networks and global access to the internet bring us amazing opportunities. Opportunities that did not exist ten years ago!

Make yourself noticed, make others seek your opinions, advice and services. Be sure you are found if someone is looking for a professional like you for a project. Did you know most Human Resource Departments google you to answer the question "Who are you"?

Market yourself; notice your work, your skills, and what you are able and willing to do. Control the information about yourself and manage it so it boosts your image! Make a name for yourself, be respected. **Be the one who decides the answer to the question "who are you?"**

That's what we call Personal Branding, a way leading to a uniquely distinguishable impression. In this book, we will see how to create and boost your Personal Brand by introducing and sharing your best qualities while creating networking.

The new battlefield for this is the social network. It's not only for companies, but for users too. All types of users. Social networks are used for everything. People have found a media where everyone expresses their views. Internet becomes a madhouse, where millions of people are connected. It's the new world, full of chaos. But **do not try to control it; adapt to it.**

So, how do we make ourselves different? And if it's possible: *Is there a way to create a good and honest personal brand without lying?* Can we do it without being a con artist?

That is what we are going to do in this book, to explore how to build our Personal Brand in an **honest and simple**

way, without lying
I encourage you all **to join me.**

GETTING STARTED

Hello there and a hearty welcome to this book, this guide about Personal Branding.

I want to take this opportunity to thank you for buying it! I hope you enjoy reading this book as much as I enjoyed writing it; and of course, thanks for taking money out of your pocket and putting it in mine.

I honestly just want you to have a good time reading. I suspect you have an idea about what we are going to talk about. Personal Branding is the translation of a social marketing strategy from enterprises to a single person. Basically, a personal branding strategy is a series of actions an individual performs to give himself value and presence in social networks by boosting his skills, strengths, knowledge and expertise. The goal: differentiate himself from the others.

We live in a very competitive world. It's no longer enough to have a degree or a masters (like 10 years ago). It's no longer a competitive advantage against another person. It's just a must.

How can we set ourselves apart? How can we get that job over so many applicants? How can we become outstanding against our competitors? Short answer (but not the easy one): differentiate ourselves. Here is where Personal Branding comes in. It will help us to achieve that goal.

WARNING: BE AWARE OF THE OGRE

Before continuing, I would like to warn you (I don't want a misunderstanding):

This book IS NOT a guide of how to learn to lie on the internet. IT IS NOT a bunch of tips about how to create a character and encourage its legend. IT IS NOT a way to stand out amongst the others by trampling on them. IT IS NOT a mantra to feed your ego and of course, IT IS NOT a guide of despicable traditional marketing techniques to scam old people.

In this book, we will see how to build an honest, humble, solid (without deception or exaggeration) personal brand, an honest way to communicate our best skills and qualities, the same qualities that make us unique. It will help us to know ourselves and better search for continuous personal self-improvement.

WHAT WILL YOU SEE IN THIS BOOK?

We are going to focus on the main existing internet tools and the correct use of them. With these tools you can achieve a remarkable personal brand whether you are looking for a professional profile or an expertise one.

First, we will see the marketing evolution over the last decade and how social marketing popped up (and therefore, Personal Branding). It's important to know where we are coming from, in order to understand where we are going, and why.

We'll see also how to set the audience and choose our target. We will plan a strategy and we learn about the "Golden Rules" of internet interactions between users.

I have a very distinctive way of writing (as you probably

have already noticed). I like simple, very direct, practical language. I love to give examples, and almost all of them (all the examples you are going to read) are based on real cases and experiences that either some my colleagues or I have gone through (I have changed names and places).

I like to use the Question-Answer style, asking very simple questions that I know are on your mind.

One of the Latin Social Marketing gurus, Gaby Castellanos, always says that the best way to deal with this stuff is to be in a good mood from the beginning. Some say that a sense of humor is a sign of intelligence; all I know is that it makes the experience nicer and more entertaining.

2 MARKETING EVOLUTION

Marketing has dramatically evolved during the last decade, a change that has been experienced by anyone under 25 years of age.

What was the turning point?

It's utterly complicated to determine it. For each country it's different. What is certain is that we can fix a moment for all them (no matter the exact year): when massive access to the internet became a reality. Do you remember the first flat-rate internet tariffs? Find in your memory the first 128k ADSL services...

WHAT DID THIS TECHNOLOGICAL IMPROVEMENT MEAN FOR MARKETING (THE TRADITIONAL STYLE)?

In order to answer this question, we have to first analyze traditional marketing. Traditional marketing was based on the idea of creating a need in the mind of the user, so you could sell him your product, which would solve his need. The technique employed was bombing ads and promotions to the public, without segmentation.

I don't care what the "great gurus of Traditional Marketing" (or let's just call them dinosaurs) said (or say, if there is still one alive); it all was based on a brute-force attack:

"If we can sell to 1 person out of every 100 people that watch our ad 30 times, let's escalate and bomb millions of them, thousands of times in several medias"
(-another dinosaur trying to justify his annual six figures).

Also:

"Let's send 20 salespeople door-to-door in the same area for the next 52 weeks. Sooner or later, they will sell something. Also, they must use tricks to scam old people, like saying, "Your neighbor already has it. Is she better than you?" or "It's an exclusive offer for you and only this week. Next week will be too late" or "Our Company only wants the best for you (and to get your pension money)".
(-the door-to-door cold selling salesman's dilemma)

And, of course, this classic:

"(It's during the evening or weekend and a call disrupted you):
- Good evening, may I talk to the lady of the house?
(...)
-... sir, your number has been generated randomly by our computer. You are not on any commercial list.
(Well, how lucky I am! I should buy a lottery ticket tomorrow! It's the 25th time I have gotten a call like that this month!)

(- The curious case of the telemarketer and the random number)[1]

All the previous **bullying** techniques are doomed to fail. All you can achieve is a high level of frustration and hatred on the part of the users toward you.

At the beginning of time, it made sense. There were not too many communication channels, so you used these methods to **make your services or products known** to the public and potential customers.

Somehow, at a certain point it changed and it became a **statistical model, based on numbers**, resulting in the scourge of traditional marketing. A disease, a virus, a parasite no longer useful. Maybe you recognize it: it's what we now call **SPAM**; and most all big companies hire spammer's services. It will never end.

So, thanks to that, all people who work in marketing (including myself), have to be tagged with this idiotic label:

"Be careful, he works in marketing... I'm sure he only wants to sell you something"

Water under the bridge. It was the past, part of the present, but for sure, not the future. The massive access to internet meant the **Big Change**. Now, when a person has a need, he looks for a solution on the internet. He is proactive. He is not only looking for different products, but he reads the opinions. He wants to see pictures, to watch videos about how it works, to have trials versions and receive free samples.

No more. Enough of saying *"my laundry detergent kills*

---

[1] To my friends from USA, you have the National Do Not Call Registry, a service offered by The Federal Communications Commission (FCC) to avoid that case. In Europe, we are screwed.

all spots. You will never see your clothes whiter," because the potential customer will go to YouTube and will check hundred of videos where former customers complain about such detergent.

The **Big Change** stops creating needs and focuses **on visibility**.

VISIBILITY

When a person has problems or needs he will start looking for a product/service that can satisfy them.

He will look at potential products that can work. He is being proactive. The results of this research will give him a short list of possible products or services. He will choose one of them. This process will guide him to what we call a **smart purchase**, and it creates the strongest relationships between the customer and the company, because it's been the customer who found the company, and not the other way around.

- Why?
- Above all, the Ego (of the customer):

"I cannot be wrong; I found it by myself after very careful research".

Are you sure? 100%? Really? Of course you were doing smart research, but don't you think that if I were a company I would be aware of what you were going to do? So, isn't there anything I could do to be sure you would find me?

Yes... that's the trick. It's not the customer who finds the Company. The Company lets the customer find him. Visibility is then, the ability of being found by your target public when they are seeking a product or service like the one you sell.

CREATION OF NEEDS

It doesn't matter who creates the need, but rather that after the customer searches for the solution, we turn out to be in his results. When he can find us, we need to offer him relevant information (as we saw before: videos, pictures, opinions, etc.) and an open dialogue (answering his questions), anything he needs to remain with us and make a smart purchase.

It isn't *"using sledgehammers to crack nuts"* anymore. Now, it's all about finding the laser-guided marketing bomb, straight to the customer, without casualties or collateral damage. It's what we call **Market Segmentation.**

MARKET SEGMENTATION

Market Segmentation involves research and location work concerning your target audience. If you have a farm with pigs, chickens and cows and you are only interested in eggs, go for the chickens. Do not check if the pigs or the cows have laid eggs. **Do not bother the other animals.** Find out where the chickens are and how to make their life better, so "they can give you" more eggs.

Thanks to segmentation and internet, a tiny SME[2] (of only 4 workers) can perform a better marketing campaign than a bigger company announced on TV.

Globalization

Buying locally is not necessary anymore. The cost reduction, the delivery time, the online payment methods and **the visibility** have changed the rules of the game. The customer doesn't care now where his purchase comes from (Berlin, Boston, Beijing or Reykjavik). The two most important things for him are that it's cheap and it arrives

---

[2] SME: Small and Medium Company

in 2-4 days. And it was all thanks to the internet.

So, how can we segment using the Internet?

The answer is simple: using the **Social Networks**.

Social Networks are the modern meeting points between people. Millions of people sign in day after day into a social network, and there are dozens and dozens of them, each one with a different and specific objective.

Economic globalization has come accompanied by **Social Globalization**, where a person not only aims to be in contact with their friends, but with their coworkers, former schoolmates, new people from other countries or just a place to flirt and hook up.

- Segmentation...

- Wait a sec, it's coming:

So when a person signs into a Social Network, he has to fill a whole profile with age, gender, what he likes, concerns, location, workplace, favorite places, movies, music, foods... The more accurate the profile is, the easier to find people who share **the same concerns and tastes.**

And in most cases, the information is real and reliable. It's not just that the user is trying to connect with people; it's also that he may want to be contacted.

Do you realize what the user is doing? He is doing **Market Segmentation**. The user himself does a segmentation based on **objective** (location, age, gender) and **subjective** (what he likes) parameters. We are getting closer to the **crux of the matter.**

Some companies saw that it was good and they said:

"Why don't we create a communication plan to reach all these users using the Social Networks? Not with a business to customer relationship, but by creating a person to person one.

Instead of using aggressive marketing techniques, why don't we just generate interesting content for our potential customers?

Why don't we set a priority to communicate with our potential customers?

And what about if we go **beyond** and we make our entire **company mission** to create experiences for the user according to **his needs,** (not ours) so he can find in us (in our services and products) that **"x factor"** he has being looking for in order to live a unique moment in a precise moment, making his experience unrepeatable?

Why, instead of selling "stuff", don't we sell unique experiences so the customer comes back over and over again trying to replicate them, trying to feel them again?

Why don't we start a SOCIAL MARKETING STRATEGY?

We have finally arrived. Social Marketing, also known as **Social Media Marketing** is the last marketing evolution, based on creating unique experiences and *person to person* communication (there are people behind a Company). Using social networks, companies are able to establish dialogues between themselves and the customers, (and potential customers) listen to them, answer their questions and develop rapid feedback[3]. This dialogue will let you know what they want, and their doubts and misunderstandings regarding your products. It's not about bombing them with promotions, discounts

---

[3] Relevant information just when it happens

or commercial communications (SPAM), it's all about **being there for them**, so when the person needs something, they **remember us.**

And for that purpose, social networks are the best media possible, because, if you lie, you are **doomed.**

How is all this related to Personal Branding? If we translate what has happened to the companies to a user level, we realize that a person can use the same channels and rules to differentiate himself from the rest.

Personal Branding is to Social Marketing as a car is to a bus. The same, but at an individual level.

Now we are talking...

3 PERSONAL BRANDING

Personal Branding is the value, the image a person projects of himself to the others. It's a perception issue:

"How do others see me? What is the image I project over them? What kind of impression do I leave? "

Creating a personal brand consists in projecting a series of values, attitudes and skills that are relevant and true. They help us to boost our strengths and give us a way to differentiate ourselves from the rest.

RELEVANCY IS SOMETHING RELATIVE.
What is relevant? Let's put some context to it. If your best skill is to ride a unicycle blindfolded while you are

doing a fire juggling performance, that skill is relevant only if you want to differentiate yourself from other circus artists in order to get a job in the circus, or if you are looking for a better dissemination of your own show.

It isn't relevant at all, however, if you are a computer designer looking for a job at Microsoft.

Despite this, your never have to discard any of your skills. You may not use the jugglery thing to impress a potential employer, but it can help you to show him the kind of person you are in your personal life. It's also a way to boost your personal brand, by humanizing the person, and not being a robot without personal opinions. You have a life, too. Use it wisely!

You need to leave an impression, and there is no way to do that without emotionally connecting with your audience. In order for people to be motivated by others, they need to share the emotional part. Remember, they are looking to empathize with you.

This is also a double-edged sword. You need to think twice about the human part of yourself you are ready to share with the rest of society.

BE AWARE OF THE OGRE

Here we are talking about the Personal Brand in a professional field. It makes no sense at all to conduct a personal branding strategy in your private life, with your family and friends. When you share with an audience some stuff about yourself, they don't care if you sleep hugging your teddy bear (unless you are a big brother participant). Similarly, your parents don't care if you can manage an ERP for international tenders. They are your parents, they love you. For them, you already have the best personal brand ever. Don't try to keep a personal brand in your private life. It will make you cocky, arrogant and unpleasant.

BE SURE YOU WANT TO MARKET YOURSELF:
In a world with so many people saying that they want to be different, it strikes me how hard they try to be the same.

We all are brands. On a professional level, if we want to boost our personal branding, we have to be conscious that we are a **commercial brand**. We need to generate real value (not fake value) and make sure our brand is associated with positive skills that make us desirable and respectable.

If you differentiate yourself from the rest, it is because you want to be **more attractive** for other people or companies. The more unique and useful you are, the greater your likelihood of being irreplaceable.

For example:
You are an engineer specialized in double use materials (for civilian and military use). It's already a good specialization, but what if you have also obtained this double use license for the US and Europe? If you succeed in letting others know what you can do, it will boost your value; you will be much more desirable for other companies working in the same field and you will gain leverage with your current company (there are not many like you, other companies want you and it's going to be hard to replace you...). So what are you waiting for? Go ahead, post articles and get involved in professional networks. Make sure, if someone searches your name, this skill is going to be attached to it.

This was a very easy example of a good skill that is worth being boosted using social media.

It's very important that you know your skills. Ask yourself the most important question:

Does it benefit or worsen my Personal Branding? And add a second part to this question: is it real or am I just making it up?

It's ok to be selective about the skills you want to promote, as long as they are real. Look, if you start with fake skills, you are always going to have this fear inside: a very rational fear of someone coming and blowing your cover.

If you are honest and you don't manipulate or make up skills you don't have, you will always have confidence when talking and communicating with people, either in real life or in social media.

QUESTION: "I've followed the traditional way and I have a good job. I'm and asset to my company and well valued in my professional environment. Why should I start a personal branding strategy if I don't need it?"

ANSWER: First of all, allow me to congratulate you. Not too many people can have that. Anyway, can I make two observations? Social media strategies aren't a substitute for traditional methods. If by following them you have achieved a very good position, imagine how much further you could go by adding an active personal branding strategy.

And the second observation: The days where people stay in the same company forever have gone away. Maybe you don't need to create a personal brand... **yet**. But, what would happen if suddenly you lost your job? Are you sure you can get another one quickly?

BE AWARE OF THE OGRE

Traditional and social strategies are not incompatible. This book is not about glorifying social media and personal branding as the only way to achieve greatness. This is just another tool, one that is very easy to manage, cheap and that goes with the rhythm of the new world. Check it out. All companies are becoming social. One of the first things you do when you meet someone is Google them (or try to find them on LinkedIn, Facebook or Twitter). The future is for whoever adapts himself to the new reality.

So far, so good. The theory and the concepts are clear. Let's check out a real life example:

THE WINE BROTHERS

John and Joseph are cousins. They have been living together since they were 18. They have also studied the same career (enology), they speak English and Spanish and both have the same professional concerns and the same work experience.

On paper, both of them have the same profile.

They go together to wine fairs, tastings, châteaux and wineries all over America (always looking to find out all the secrets of the new elixirs of the god **Bacchus[4]**).

They really enjoy these experiences. They were born for them. It's not only on a personal level, but in a professional way too. It's all about going, commenting, changing impressions, meeting people, taking pictures and

---

[4] Bacchus is the Roman name for Dionysus, the god of wine and intoxication

flirting with the hostesses.

John **has a blog**, titled "The pilgrim taster". Every time he goes to a wine event, he **writes a new post**. In that post he talks about the wines he has tasted and his impressions. He loads pictures, videos, interviews with winemakers, gives references to find out more about the event, and also gives his conclusion. He **answers questions** from the readers and his followers. He uses his **twitter account** during the event as a way of providing "breaking news" of the event, **sharing** what's going on and using the official Hashtag of the event.

Joseph doesn't have a blog, or twitter, just a Facebook profile where he uploads his pictures. John also has his Facebook profile.

They both upload pictures and videos before, during and after the event (when they are partying, too). They are young and attractive boys with a lot of success. The pictures... well, let's say their "ethylic states" are not the best.

The difference is that John posts all these pictures privately, only sharing them with some of their friends. Joseph doesn't care. He doesn't mind privacy issues; "who cares, right?"

So, coming back to a professional level, is there any difference? Is John a better tester than Joseph? They are going to these events for the same reasons: fun, professional concerns, willing to learn more, wine love and party love.

But, what would happen if a winemaker were looking for a promoter for his wines? If he receives a résumé from each one and he decides to investigate them (or Google them) a bit, it wouldn't be difficult to find these differences:

Although both of them travel a lot to many places in

America to attend wine events, John is the only one talking about that on the Internet.

John seems to be plenty immersed in these events. He knows people and has interviewed winemakers. The potential boss can check these interviews and the potential level of knowledge he has about the wine market.

He does find pictures of the events from Joseph, but it's seems he is just a spoiled child always partying and drunk at these events

Bottom-line for the winemaker, **John is a professional; Joseph isn't**. But is it really true? Not at all. The only difference is that John is carrying on a personal branding strategy to become an honest and respectful professional in his field. John decides to sacrifice part of his time in social networking and writing posts. He shares content, answers questions, dialogues with his followers and increases his networking. John boosts his professional life and keeps for himself his private one. The result: he looks like a legitimate wine professional.

Joseph, on the other hand, because of his lack of concern, looks irresponsible and careless. Although, he can do the same job as John...

... if you were the winemaker, who would you hire?

This is probably an extreme example, but not unusual. Unfortunately, our social impact is one of the factors employers are taking into account these days when they are hiring.

Don't worry, there are some simple golden rules that are very easy to follow if you want to work on your personal branding image.

4 FIVE GOLDEN RULES

Burn them in your memory. They are very important for a successful Personal Branding Strategy.

1ˢᵀ *BE POLITE*

The words "please" and "thanks" are not going to bite you; trust me. It's very basic. So take a moment and check your emails and online messages (omit your dear friends if you want, but check "formal" emails)... Maybe it is because we want to save time (typing thanks and please takes a lot of it), or maybe we think online communication is direct, straight to the crux of the matter, so we forget about the form and focus on the content... **rubbish**! It's just bad manners.

Not so long ago, an email from a post graduate student

arrived in my inbox. She was writing about the meat market in the UK. A few months earlier I had published a market research report for the Spanish Foreign Trade Institute (ICEX) about the meat and meat products market in the UK.

So, the student contacted me, asking for help. I'm going to copy word for word that email (well, I have translated it):

Good afternoon,

I'm RS, a student of the Post Graduate Degree XXXXXXXX. My work team and I are doing a final project regarding a Spanish Company that produces chicken meat (TARIC YYYYYY) and wants to export to the UK (it's an internationalization project). We've seen you have a document published about that.

We would like to ask you for some information so we can do the work more accurately:

1.- Logistics Operators in the UK
2.- A list of Spanish Companies that already export to the UK
3.- Agents and salesmen (or a way to contact them)

And in general, it will be very useful whatever information you may have regarding the meat market in the UK (focusing on the chicken meat market)

Greetings,
RS

Let me begin by saying that when you translate to English, this email loses some meaning. So, allow me to point this out:

In Spanish (as with other Latin languages) there are two

forms of talking to a person. You can use an informal way (in Spanish, "Tú", which is the second person singular verb conjugation) and a formal way (the third person of the singular verb conjugation, "Usted"). Well this mail was written in a very informal way (using the Tú). The same way you would talk to your brother or a dear friend.

All right. Let's do an emotional intelligence exercise. I am not particularly vain, but... was this the best way to ask for help? Back then, I was no longer working for the Foreign Trade Institute. I had a new job with tons of obligations and no time at all. From her point of view I was a reputed professional.   Why should I answer someone I had never met? Please, read the email again and notice that there is not a single "please", or a "thanks in advance". Again, why should I or anyone answer an impolite email?

I didn't answer the email. **She wasn't worth it.** Remember:

DEMAND - DEMAND - DEMAND -> NO

EMPATHIZE - BE POLITE – BE GRATEFUL ->
YES

2ND DO NOT CRITICIZE

Allow me to make a clarification: Do not criticize if you don't provide content.

Of course you can participate in a debate and criticize something if you do it in a **constructive manner**. When you just criticize without arguments, you are being an internet "**troll**", and people hate that. The best is to expose your concerns; you are a **person with concerns** and you ask to solve them. It's based on the Socratic Method. Socrates' favorite phrase was, "and why is that?". Using this method, you are approaching people, asking them about what they say, showing them that although you are not completely in agreement with what they say, you are not against it, and you want to understand their point of view.

This starts an **emotional conversation**; you are open to new suggestions, you want to understand them and you establish a dialogue. You are **open-minded** (or maybe not, but just pretend to be. I'm quite sure the moment you give it a chance, you will end up enjoying it).

Do not criticize if the conversation isn't going your way, because it provokes a reaction of **"who died and left you in charge"**. People don't want to connect with *a little know-it-all*, who always needs to have the last word.

Please, do not use the expression **"with all due respect, I believe…"**. The person, who listens that, in his mind, hears this:

"With all due respect, I don't give a s*. You don't know what you are talking about; listen to me, because I'm the supreme truth-holder. Named by God himself".

If your goal is **networking**, find collaborations or simply, make yourself known, learn to have emotional intelligence. If you don't follow the advice above, you will create a very negative reputation for yourself. In real life, a bad first impression can still be solved (with a lot of effort). In the digital world, it cannot be.

Let me give you an example of how it happened to me:

In one of my articles (in the comments section), a

person asked me about my bibliography. I wrote him back with some books he could read. Well, the problem was he wrote biography instead bibliography, and I used biography as bibliography too. A **lapsus calami**[5], an honest mistake.

Well, a third person (let's call him MS) not involved in the conversation wrote:

"You don't know how to write very well, and you misunderstand terms like biography and bibliography.

FT20 is a website where I publish free guides and articles about foreign trade, and I also respond to questions. It's a nonprofit website and the aim is just to help people with international commerce proceeds.

Honestly, it felt like a kick in the chest. Ask yourselves: Was the comment from MS necessary? Was it in context? Do you believe it was the best way to point out a mistake?

Please, be constructive. Look for the dialogue instead of the argument. Ask others about their thoughts instead of trying to convince them of yours.

3ᴿᴰ THINK BEFORE YOU ACT.

As human beings, we are impulsive by nature. Many people say the first thing that comes to their minds, and they called it **spontaneity.** In the day to day, it's not a big deal, but in the digital world, spontaneity is also known as **"self-immolation"**.

When you are with your friends, you can say a lot of stupidities that they won't tell in public. It's normal; when you are with your friends it's different than with strangers.

Our friends know we are joking... but strangers may

---

[5] It's a Latin expression that means an involuntary and unconscious mistake when writing.

not. That's why we are more polite, educated and we think before acting when we are at work, in a conference, with a client or with our father in law.

So, why is it so hard for so many people to think before acting? Look at twitter. How many people write truly idiotic tweets they wouldn't say in public? Why are they being so impulsive? Well, it's a form of liberation. They are anonymous, so they can yell and be mad. They are barking dogs...

If you are working on your personal branding, from now on, be smart, think about what you are going to say before you say it. Ask yourself:

Does it help me?
Is it important and relevant?
Is what I'm going to say real and honest?

Think twice, and if the answers to all three of the previous questions are yes, then go ahead.

If you still have a few doubts, just go to sleep. I'm not kidding. In the evening, our mind is tired. It's hard to think clearly; **reflecting overnight** is the best thing you can do. It could be that a comment you want to publish late at night is a **massive weapon of destruction** in the early morning. And once it's been thrown, there is no going back.

4ᵀᴴ BE ASSERTIVE

Assertiveness is the art of denying a statement while letting the other person believe they are right. It's the skill of being confident without being aggressive. Let me give you an example:

David goes with Carla (his girlfriend) to an expensive restaurant. It's a big night for him, he is going to propose to her. For the main dish, he orders a steak, but when the waiter serves it, it's uncooked. So David asks him to take back the steak and cook it a little bit. But, the waiter says: "Bite me! The steak is perfectly cooked".

Now, what will David do?

A: What did you say? Keep your food, we are leaving.
Date ends, moment gets ruined, and she won't be in the best mood if David proposes to her.

B: I don't f* care about your opinion. Bring the steak the way I asked for it.
David shows himself to be dominant and aggressive. All alpha. The waiter will bring back the dish as David ordered, but it's quite possible, that like an Easter egg, it will have a surprise inside (but not a fun one). Would you risk eating the steak?

C: Ok, don't worry; I will eat it like that.
David does nothing, and eats the raw steak. David is paying for something he doesn't want to eat, but he doesn't want any problems. He's being weak in front of his future fiancée.

D: You are right. She also says that to me... all the time! So I'm sorry to insist, but can you tell the chef to cook it a little more, please? Thanks.
David has been clever; he has been assertive. He's been calm, and funny. He turned a potentially unpleasant situation into a funny anecdote. He let the waiter be right and he can be sure no one is going to spit in his steak when it comes back. He has been neither weak nor

dominant, but in the end, he has his well cooked steak and nobody is angry.

When we break the first rule (be polite), we can find ourselves in situations we don't understand very well. "Why is he reacting like that?" Being assertive will help us resolve these kinds of situations. Who knows? Maybe this person is having a bad day. Maybe the waiter found out that he was going to be fired after his shift.

Being assertive is better than burning a bridge forever.

5TH NEVER LIE

This is the most important one. It seems stupid and basic. I beg you; keep it well engraved in your memory.

Lies could save you temporarily, but for sure, not forever. It's bread for today, hunger for tomorrow.

Boosting your personal brand using lies is a massive mistake. If others find out your lies (and they will, trust me), there is no going back. You will lose your credibility.

Picture this: you are talking about and publishing your experience in Africa as a missionary. It's a lie. You've never been there, but you are gaining a lot of followers and respect. It would be very complicated for someone to discover your lie.

Well, imagine now, because the world is small enough to fit in a pocket, that someday, someone from the place you claim you've been connects with you and your followers...

Tick, tock...

A friend of mine once told me he witnessed a woman interrupt the office of an independent consultant he was going to meet. She shouted that this man was a liar and that he should be ashamed of himself. She cursed the day she met him.

My friend was shocked. Obviously, he preferred to wait to hire the man until he found out more about him. He turned out to be a real fraud. He was lying about former customers, studies, projects, and who knows what else. He lost a potential customer and gained a bad reputation in my friend's contact network.

Do not lie. If you do (we all are humans, and we can fail), be proactive. Apologize; ask if there is anything you can do to compensate the possible damage. Be humble and learn for the next time.

5 NETWORKING

Social networks have a huge capacity to communicate our thoughts, ideas, works and any other things we want to share. The problem is that most of the users are yelling. Nobody listens. We all want to talk and be heard, but we hardly listen to what others have to say.

The Personal Branding Strategy cannot be based on a "me-me-me" concept. It needs to be a "me-you-us" approach. Building a personal brand is an individual work, but you are always going to be playing in a collective court. You need to interact with other people and professionals with your same concerns.

ASK YOURSELF THESE 3 QUESTIONS:

What could my contribution be (what are you good at)?
How could other people's contributions be good for me (what are they good at)?
How can I connect with them (how can we share what

each one is good at)?

Once you understand it's pointless to boost your personal brand if it's not going to have an impact, you will realize how important it is to create a contacts network in order to disseminate your content. This network will help you to differentiate yourself in what you are really good at, share your content and be respected for that.

It is a two-way street. You get help and you give help. Remember what Mike Tyson said: "I prefer to give than to receive".

Sharing other people's content won't make you look weak (unless that is all you do). It will make you better, because you will also listen.

And when you start listening, you can start commenting and interacting. Other people will do the same with you, and you will **create bonds**.

This network creation is called **Networking**.

Networking is the net of relationships you build; these are the people you connect with in order to learn and share content (created by you or by them).

Remember, **you are not alone.** You cannot be heard if you don't listen first. To be a source of information, you need to be informed of everything that is going on.

The good thing about Networking is not only that you are going to look for people, but people are going to look for you too.

Q: Why? Why is Networking so important?
A: It opens doors.

One of them is the **information door.** The bigger network you create, the more information you can get. It will help you to keep posted on current events. Being in the loop allows you to participate in the debate, and share opinions and news.

Another door is **the reference door**. No one listens anymore to the lonely hermit that comes once a year from his retirement to give a speech from a mound about the end of the world. You cannot be a reference only by yourself. You become a reference also by the people you are connected to. You need to be good by yourself and also be good by the people you are associated with. You cannot do it without networking.

And, maybe, the most important: **the job door.** Check out companies' human resources market. Almost all companies are SME (small and medium-sized enterprises). When a job opportunity arises, the first question the boss asks the employees is always the same:

"Do you know someone that could fit in this profile?"

It's simple, small companies don't have human resources departments. So they always ask first before struggling with other ways to hire the person they need. Besides, when you are looking for a job, if you have any connection in a medium or large company, this person can help you out in many ways: first, by letting you know there is an open process or a job opportunity, then with human resources, (how to talk to them, what do they want to hear, questions they are going to ask, etc.) and finally, even by recommending you to their bosses:

"I've been following this guy; his work is good. He knows about what we do and he can do it".

Maybe, you are not looking for a job, but networking **will bring you business opportunities**:

- *"Do you know someone that can do this?"*
- *"Hey mate, the other day someone asked me about a product I don't sell, but I thought of you, because you do sell it! Here is the contact".*

Never belittle the strength of a good Network.

Q: Is Networking hard to create?
A: Not at all.

There is only one rule: **be honest**. People hate con artists and liars. If they catch you in a lie, they won't forgive you. It's nasty when another person tells you "you are a fraud". And it's even worse if it's true.

Q: Where do I begin?
A: Networking is about being social.

It's part of your personal branding strategy. In the following chapters, we are going to see how to start, how to choose the audience and how to select the different networks. Networking will come automatically with every step you take. Don't worry; it's very easy and pleasant.

6 STARTING A PERSONAL BRANDING STRATEGY

BE AWARE OF THE OGRE

I don't want you to think I'm some kind of guru, or even worse, that I'm the only one with the key of knowledge. The guide we are going to see is just my point of view. The way I learned it. It is just a very simple and very practical guide you can follow to start and pursue a Personal Branding Strategy.

There are many other ways. Each one has its own method. If you are already an expert on self-marketing, you probably won't learn anything new (or only a couple of things, maybe). **This book is for the person that is starting now.** The only thing I hope to be is fun, easy to read and really helpful.

So far, we have seen a general picture of **today's marketing**: the new social marketing wave, the personal branding and the modern Networking. It's time to roll up our sleeves and start designing our **Personal Branding Strategy.**

Before we begin, here are three major questions you need to reflect on:

1. What do I have now? Am I in any social networks? What am I doing on them? **(Current situation)**

2. What do I want to become? Where do I want to be in the future? What do I expect to achieve? **(Long term)**

3. What results would I like to achieve in a year from now? **(Short-medium term)**.

Remember, depending on your goals, you may need to use the tools we are going to see with more or less intensity. Please, do yourself a favor and set **realistic objectives in accordance with your potential and your skills**.

It's better to set simple goals at the beginning than establish goals you will never be able to reach.

Groucho Marx once said: "Happiness is made of **little things:** a little yacht, a little mansion, a little fortune..."

CHOOSING YOUR AUDIENCE

This is the trickiest part of your strategy. It's a question only you can answer.

Choosing an audience doesn't mean that the audience is going to follow you right away. It means, you are going to create content focused on them. As we have said before, if the content is good, eventually, it will start to be valued.

Let's look at the most common scenario: **work.**

If you are looking for a job, first, you need to ask yourself if you want to create your own company or you want to work for someone else. If it's the first option, your audience is going to be your potential clients on one hand, and professionals from your complementary sectors on the other. They could be helpful to you if you need certain jobs to be done.

For example:

If you want to mount your own eco farm, you should connect to lawyers specialized in fresh products legislation. Their knowledge may help you.

If you want to be employed by others, your audience must be (mostly) experts in your field; it doesn't matter if it's the same sector or not. For example, if you are a music teacher, other experts will be other teachers. No need for them to be music teachers, too. The idea is that, thanks to them, you can be updated on teaching techniques or news in education (like vacancies in schools).

There are more scenarios. For example:

Who?	Audience	Goal
University students	Teachers, colleagues, multidisciplinary experts	New trends, internships, collaborations for class works.
Post degree students	Colleagues, teachers, sector experts, complementary sectors	First professional relationships, job, expertise in a particular sector.
Job seekers	Human resources companies, people with concerns in the same field, sources of information and private companies from relevant sector.	Show talent, work, feedback, new trends, and job opportunities.
Public servants	Other public administrations and companies. People in the same work field.	Help others; transmit public offers to the private market. Information about opportunities in the public sector, changes and new laws

A very practical example:

WHO	AUDIENCE	WHY? GOALS
Fitness Monitor	Gym users, fitness centers of his area and regions nearby. Foreign experts in fitness, fitness brands and companies	Self marketing, so he can be called by other gyms in the area. Reputation of a good instructor. Knowing the market trends. Applying them... "He's an expert, a very good professional and we are happy to have him here" (future employer thought).

BE AWARE OF THE OGRE

There is one last thing you need to know about this. You must position yourself. This means you **cannot be loved by all.** It's impossible. Inside your audience, you will find people that think differently than you, and you shouldn't change what you want to say (or not say it) because you are going to upset them. Use the five rules we've seen, but be aware, **you will have to defend your position, and most of the time, it will be impossible to please everyone.**

7 SET PREVIOUS MATERIAL

You've already set your goals and decided your audience. Now is the moment to implement it. We are going to prepare the material we need to begin.

PUBLIC PICTURE

You can only give a first impression once. What's it going to be like? It's of utmost importance to choose a good profile picture. It will be the first impression, the cover of our book, our introduction. A bad one will create unconscious antagonism.

<u>Tips for your public picture</u>

Be natural:
When taking a photo, ask your friends to be there with you. Have fun, make some jokes, relax and chill out with them. Do you know why? Because you want to look

genuinely happy. And the best way to do that is by **being happy**.

Be accessible:

Do not cross your arms. It gives the impression you are not willing to embrace new challenges, people, feelings or situations, etc.

Be loyal to yourself:

You have to find your own style and be loyal to it. Of course if your objective is to work for a large white collar company you should keep a certain dress code, but remember: your personal brand depends on you, and only you.

If you feel confident in a suit, wear it. If you feel yourself wearing a military jacket and a fedora, go ahead! And if you don't believe me, check for example Hank Blank (Google him). He is possibly one of the best "self-marketing" teachers in the world, and he has his very own style without looking less professional. Sometimes a creative photo leaves a stronger impression.

Don't fake it:

The most important thing in the photo is YOU, not the place the picture is being taken. You are what matters; you want people to focus on you, not the views.

Of course you can Photoshop it, but not too much. It's best to just adjust simple things like light or contrast. Do not fake it. Accept your age and your wrinkles, moles and scars. Accepting them without hesitation means you are confident and happy with yourself. Is there anything more important?

Ask your friends:

Take more than one or two pictures... as many as you

can! Even if you think you've already got it. Then, the fun part comes: tell your friends to choose one. That's right; it's not going to be you, but other people who choose your picture. Ask them, "how does it feel", "what are the sensations", "any irrational feelings", and very important "what does it transmit". Let them do a short list, and choose wisely according to the message you want to give and the skills it transmits.

Smile!

Maybe the most important thing: SMILE, smile and smile! If you are not used to smiling in pictures, takes thousands of them until you get used to it and it will become natural. Whenever you see a camera, smile.

EXPERT RÉSUMÉ VS. CHRONOLOGICAL RÉSUMÉ

A (reverse) **chronological résumé** lists your job experiences in reverse chronological order. A "correct" one should cover your last 5 to 10 years (including your training). It's a good type of résumé if you are a *newborn*, a brand *new deer* coming from University without professional experience.

The trouble comes when you already have professional experience; you've been working in a few companies in different fields and you have carried out a couple of projects. You cannot use a chronological résumé anymore. You need to go for an **Expert Résumé.**

An expert résumé is focused on a specific area. It's more complex and functional than a chronological résumé. The aim is to show all your experience regarding a certain field.

That means not only professional experience and training, but also publications, collaborations, networks and skills.

This type of resume is the best way to show people the problems (or challenges) you've experienced and how you've come out of them.

Tell your story. Make it palpable and convey your feelings. You are a real person that has been in the same situation that the person who is reading the résumé is in right now, and you sorted it out!

That's an expert!

Question: I don't have very much experience or training. Does that mean I can only use a chronological résumé?

Answer: You don't have these things, YET. However, you can, and you should do an Expert Résumé.

Personal branding is not built in a day. It's a long journey of constant improvements. You may not yet have the perfect expert résumé, but I'm quite sure you have had some problems, and that you have solved them. It's doesn't matter if it's a summer job or homework for the University, the important thing is that it shows your abilities and skills.

There also some tricks:

If you lack professional experience, go deeply into your training, your professional training. One of the biggest mistakes of recently graduated students is to think they don't have any experience... And what about the last 3 or 5 years?

Use the Expert Résumé to make it clear you have the knowledge and the willingness. The feeling you need to transmit is that *you are ready, you are passionate, you can't wait to have an opportunity and you won't fail.*

If you lack training, but not experience, emphasize the knowledge you've acquired just by working. Your *differential factor* is the *know-how* an expert can only get by working. The point is, that even if you don't have a masters degree or specific training regarding a certain skill set, *you want to learn; you want to know more and more about it.*

No EXP points, no training. You have your concerns! You want to learn. Your goal is to be better tomorrow, starting today. Experts are made, not born!

Good results are rarely achieved in the short term. Ask yourself, starting now, where will you be in one year? Or two?

The Expert Résumé is the base of our social profile. It's dynamic and organic. It evolves. The network and our publications will help us to improve it and fill the gaps of experience and training.

CONTACT INFO

Public life is different from private life. The two can converge at a particular moment in time, but usually, they don't.

Where you draw the line in the sand between your public and your private life is up to you, as are the ways in which you can be contacted.

In any case, there is basic contact information you need to have. Let's see it.

Basic Contact Info.

Contact email: get an email where you can be contacted, an email for your public brand. It's the first step in our Personal Branding Strategy. Please, do not use Hotmail. Hotmail is forbidden. It's not serious and people may think it's SPAM. You can use your Google account to get a Gmail address. It can also be used to sign in to other applications: Google drive, Google Plus, YouTube, Google

Analytics, etc.

Create a Skype Username. Skype is the most used program for calls and video calls between computers. If you don't want to give a phone number, this can be an alternative.

I know it's tempting, but avoid using strange usernames or nicknames like *"teddybear89"*, *"badboy69"*, *"bigjoe"* and so on. Remember, be serious and clean. Use your name and surname. If necessary, you can also use your middle name or a combination of all of them.

Suggested:

In addition to your Gmail address, get your own domain. It's cheap and you can have your custom email address. Also, you can host a simple website about you and your work. Remember, you are a professional and you are working on your personal brand using social media. **It's a must to have your own domain**. If you buy a domain, also pay for hosting (space to create and host your website).

A dedicated phone number where you can receive calls regarding your professional and public profile.

Paper and electronic business cards.

8 SOCIAL NETWORKS

Social networks give us very important information in real time. Thanks to them, we can connect with our friends or people with our same concerns. When we are developing our personal brand, it's very important to decide who to follow and where. Not all social networks are used the same way. Each one has its own rules and objectives. **So, which one should you choose?**

It depends on three factors: **the audience** you want to reach, **the content** you are going to share, and the **specific social network goals**.

We've already looked at how to choose your audience, and also the questions you need to ask yourself in order to find out what are you good at, and what you want to share (content). Let's put all of this in context with choosing social networks.

For example:

If you are a photographer specialized in weddings, it's highly recommended to be on Tumblr, Flickr or Instagram (**content**)
If you make hand-made accessories/jewelry and are trying to gain female customers, you must be on Pinterest (**audience**)
If you are a logistics manager looking for a job, LinkedIn is your place (**goal**)

Basically, all social networks are divided in three groups:
- **Horizontals**: they give general interrelationship.
- **Vertical by user**: targeting a particular audience.
- **Vertical by activity:** focused on a particular activity.

Type	Activity	Name
Horizontal	General interrelationship. Sharing all types of content for all kinds of purposes.	**Facebook**
Vertical by user	The audience is professional workers. People who want to promote, find a job, collaborations or do new business.	**LinkedIn**
Vertical by activity	Microblogging. All kinds of people sharing the same way, less than 140 characters	**Twitter**

Let's see each one's pros, cons and best uses.

FACEBOOK

Facebook is a leisure network. It started with the aim to connect people from the same college, and it evolved into a way to connect with friends and former classmates.

Little by little, it's starting to change, and now it's also a place where companies try to connect with their customers (or potential customers) to offer them content, promotions and updates.

What defines Facebook?

The main difference is that the user chooses the people that are going to form his "friends circle". This means that if I want to follow and get in contact with you (for example), I need you to approve it. So you are in control of who is following you.

Latest updates included privacy tools that allowed the user to set different grades of access: friends, acquaintances and others (defined by the user himself). So publications target different audiences (according to this filter tool).

Facebook has the largest number of users. You can publish pictures, comments, videos, enquiries, links to other publications, play applications, join groups and many more.

But at the end of the day, Facebook is mostly used for two things: sharing moods and loading pictures about parties, travels or selfies. So...

Is it the best social network to boost your personal brand?

Personal branding gets associated with public and professional life. Facebook mixes it with private life, too. This is not entirely bad, because it is a way to share some aspects of our personality in order to reinforce our brand.

Question: Isn't it a bad idea, to carry out a personal branding strategy amongst our friends?

Answer: You are not carrying out a strategy with your friends. It's for all the other people you are going to find in this network. One of the worst things employees have to face is when their bosses send them a friend request on Facebook. *"What can I do?"* It's a lose-lose situation, unless you elaborate a personal branding strategy. *What do you want to share? With who? Why? How does it help you?*

Q: If someone asks me, I can tell him I don't have a Facebook profile. End of story.

A: It's not that easy. Even if you do not have a Facebook profile, other people expect you to have one. So if they cannot find it, they get suspicious. What is he/she hiding?

Why use this network?

We've seen the two main motives. First of all, everyone expects you to have a profile. Secondly, if we are smart, we can use this network to let people know (strangers and acquaintances alike) *the values about ourselves we want them to know.*

What information should you share?

Here is where we go back to your personal branding strategy. You defined skills, values and capabilities. Share content that goes in line with that. You need to be consistent. Same rules apply as before (be polite, do not criticize, think before you act, be assertive and do not lie).

What you can never do or share

For your private circle you can do whatever you want. Let's get focused when you post public content. You never know who will read it, so, don't post religious, political or controversial comments. Don't post during work time (if you are working). You are supposed to be working, not hanging out on a social network. Never talk bad about your current or former company. Don't insult and don't lose your manners. If you have hesitations about what you are going to post, don't post it.

Some top tips you need to know to use Facebook as a tool for your personal branding strategy:

Develop different lists: best friends, friends, acquaintances, strangers, workmates, former colleagues, business contacts, etc. You can determine what information each one can see. This is crucial.

Privacy: by default, set all your publications with the most restrictive privacy filter, and then choose which ones you want to make public.

Don't let anyone label you in pictures without your approval. When someone tries to tag you, your approval will be needed in order to add it to your timeline.

Respect other's privacy. Change your configuration so only your friends can see your connections.

Be careful about the pages you "like". Most of the time they are friends' suggestions and you don't realize what they are about.

Set that only friends can write on your timeline.

There are thousands of privacy guides about Facebook. Read at least one.

Armoring your Facebook profile

Is it fair to have to share our social and private Facebook profile just because not doing so can harm us?

Absolutely not. It's highly unfair. Luckily for you, there is a solution. Create a public and professional Facebook profile and hide the personal for friends.

We can use the public profile for our co-workers, bosses, potential employers and people we have the obligation to add to our circle but don't want to.

The trick is eliminating any trace of our private profile from the research engines and instead positioning our public one. How?

Follow these steps:

- For your personal profile, use an alias, or your name without surnames. A combination of the surnames may work too (if it's not pretty obvious). Your friends will recognize you, but it will be complicated for strangers.
- There is an option in privacy you can mark so that nobody can find you by your email address. Mark it.
- Delete information about where you are living (your friends already know), where you studied, your work history and contact information (phone, email, Skype, etc.)
- Set private publications by default.
- Be sure your personal profile is not linked to any other website.
- Create a public profile linked to your public email. Use name and surname.
- Fill academic and work fields.
- Use your public contact info.
- Introduce a link to your public Facebook profile on other websites (your website, other public profiles you

have, etc.).

- Keep it up to date, so it looks like it's being regularly used.

TWITTER

Twitter is a microblogging social network. People direct ideas in short messages (140 characters tops). These messages are called **tweets**.

Whilst on Facebook you define your friend circle, on Twitter the people decide if they will follow you or not. You don't have any control unless you protect your tweets (in this case, whoever wants to follow you will need your permission).

Information found on Twitter will be relevant or not depending on the nature of the person (or institution) that tweets it and their reliability (as with any other information source).

You can see in realtime *what's going on*: the trends. Trends can be national (for the country you want) or international. To classify the information and find out the trends, Twitter uses an interest tags system called **Hashtags.** A Hashtag is a word or a term that defines the idea behind the tweet. It's written with the "#" before. For example, to check out what people are saying about personal branding, type *#personalbranding* in the twitter search engine. You will see all tweets (ordered by date) that used that particular Hashtag.

Similarly, the "@" sign followed by a username is used for mentioning or replying to other users.

Why use this network?
Twitter offers information and access to international experts in your field. If you want to keep in the loop, use this network to find all kind of information regarding one

topic.

It helps you to identify references in your sector, and grants you access to content shared by people from all around the world. Remember what we said, an expert is not a hermit, isolated from society; it's a well informed person, with connections and social skills.

Also, Twitter is a realtime information source. Let me give you an example. During the Arab Spring (2011), official information coming from Egypt was subjected to censorship. Without social networks, and Twitter mostly, it would have been impossible for the world to get the whole picture about what was going on. We gained information not only through the tweets, but also through the pictures, videos and sounds recorded and posted. Thousands of people were tweeting about the riots, the police response, the incidents... It was a realtime event followed by millions of people using a 140 characters system.

What information should you share?
The rules are the same as for Facebook. Actually, when we use the social networks for our personal branding strategy, we need to follow the five golden rules.

140 character tweets force you to write very relevant and direct information. If you share uninteresting comments, people won't follow you (and may also unfollow you).

Share links to your articles, or to other networks where you have content: videos on YouTube or Vine, designs on Pinterest or pictures on Instagram.

Start a conversation with other followers and dialogue. Retweet (RT) relevant information (retweeting is when a tweet is forwarded via Twitter by users). If you use information from another user, remember to mention him/her (using the @).

What type of information can you share?

Twitter is not only used to post comments or moods, but short conversations, pictures, videos, links to blogs, news and all kind of content. Basically, whatever you want to share becomes a link.

When you upload a video or a picture, it's Twitter itself who creates the shortest link possible. But it doesn't do the same with external links. That's why it's very important to shorten the links. With this purpose, there are websites that offer this service for free. One of the most popular is bitly.com. If you register you can also keep track of the people that click on the link.

What should you never do?

Don't use it as a way to get things off your chest and out of your system. Because of the anonymity, Twitter is highly used for people to express authentic nonsense and absurdities, **sometimes true atrocities**. If you want an anonymous Twitter account, go ahead and create an account with a nickname, but don't use your public one.

Very important: **Sometimes less is more.** One tweet a day is better than many irrelevant tweets throughout the whole day. You are in danger of being considered a spammer by your followers. They may unfollow you, or worse, hide your updates, so that you will have the false sense of being interesting. Never write a mentions tweet. How to identify these tweets: someone suddenly mentions you (and 5 others) in the same tweet. This user is just trying to increase his number of followers.

Twitter lists

You can create twitter lists (private or public). The lists

help you to group followers and people you are following. You can classify them using your own criteria. For example, you can create a list called personal branding and add to that list all of the people you follow that talk about that topic. Or you can create one list for institutions and another for people. The point is to group them, so you won't miss information.

Although lists can be public (and most of them are), I highly recommend you create four private lists that you will use in your daily personal branding strategy:

- Followers (they follow you)
- People you follow that you want to become your followers (so you can retweet them, participate when they start a conversation, etc.)
- Best followers (people that follow you and interact with you)
- Experts in your sector that share good content (so you can share it too)

Lists will help you to share good content produced in your environment. It's an easy way to quickly check your followers' publications and increase engagement with them by sharing the most interesting ones.

People who interact with us are good followers. Using a list you can have all their publications separated. It's like paying special attention to them.

Remember, we all want to give our opinion and be listened to (and shared). So it's very normal to feel *disappointed when no one shares our publication, even if it is* the best article we've ever written. This happens because we don't share.

Get used to checking your lists and selecting the best content. Dialogue with other users and listen to what they have to say.

How to increase the number of followers

Somehow, increasing the number of followers is the top concern of personal branding gurus. The most common way (without buying them) is to follow a high number of twitter users, hoping a percentage of them (5-10%) will follow you as well. After that, you unfollow all of them and start the cycle again (but you gained a few users).

This is a very unpleasant way to increase the number of followers. It's a horrible strategy that I don't recommend.

Remember that an important part of gaining followers is based on elaborating good content they feel happy to share. Twitter has so many users, that getting noticed is a problem. You can follow these steps:

- Start by identifying and following references in your sector and institutions. Use the Hashtags to find who talks about what.
- Check their followers, to find people like you (with your same concerns) and follow them, too.
- Interact with them. Not only mark their publications as favorites, but also retweet them and most importantly, talk to them. (Do not get in the middle of an already existing conversation between two users; you may get the opposite effect you were looking for).
- Once they follow you (if they do), keep the contact, check their news and interact with them.
- Follow who really follows you.
- Repeat the process with your followers' followers.

No rush and please, do not unfollow them the moment they start following you. If so, you are going to have a huge number of followers, but with low engagement. By targeting the correct audience, you can have more and better followers.

Create your own Hashtag

Create a Hashtag for your topics. A phrase or a **hint**[6] that no one else uses. It will be part of your personal branding strategy. It needs to be easy to remember and as short as possible.

LINKEDIN

LinkedIn is a social network created for professionals. This network connects professionals from different companies, sectors and fields. It's an online résumé, but it's not just the digital version of a paper one. It goes beyond.

LinkedIn offers a personal profile page, that the user fills with all the relevant information that he wants. This can include professional expertise, academic formation, attached files (paper résumé, videos, pictures), projects, publications, volunteers, edited books, skills, recommendations from former bosses (or current ones) and any other information the user thinks is relevant.

For personal branding purposes, it's imperative to have a public profile here.

LinkedIn brings us the possibility to connect with people from our own sector around the world. It's the perfect tool for networking, and as we saw before, networking is a top priority for our strategy.

What are the main features of LinkedIn?

---

[6] A **hint** in Personal Branding is a slogan that defines what you are, what you offer and what your philosophy is. It's short and unique. For example, I have two: "plan your present, design your future" (mine) and "finding ways or creating them" (derivate from Hannibal's quote *"I will either find a way, or make one"*).

We can find four major features. The first one is the most basic: **creating a professional profile**. With this profile, you can contact other professionals by sending them a request (or by accepting requests sent to you). LinkedIn also supports the formation of **interest groups**. Groups are a discussion area. They can be private, accessible to members only or may be open to internet users in general. The majority of the largest groups are employment related. The **job listings** are the third important feature. Companies post job offers, and they all get ordered and classified by LinkedIn. You can check jobs by company, by country, by city or by using key words. Also, because it's LinkedIn, you are able to see if people from a certain company are connected and try to contact them for assessment. The last feature added: **Influencers**. LinkedIn offers you some of the world's top thought leaders. They share posts about their professional insights with LinkedIn's members. These leaders come from a vast range of industries.

What can you do on LinkedIn?

You can create your profile in other languages. LinkedIn will check the IP of the visitor (to know where they are coming from) and will display your profile in the same language as theirs (if you have a profile in that particular language).

LinkedIn allows users to endorse each other's skills. This feature also allows users to efficiently provide commentary on other users' profiles.

You can ask for recommendations.

You can upload files to your profile, so they are available for your contacts (presentations, videos, and pdfs). This is the perfect way to complete your profile (with a video resume, for example).

LinkedIn can create a résumé in pdf format from your profile.

You can add your motivation letter.

You can link your LinkedIn profile with your Twitter account. So every publication you make will show up on your twitter, too.

Rules to use LinkedIn
Basically there are **two rules**.

First Rule: When you are going to contact someone you've never met before, include a tiny motivation letter in the request. Why do you want to connect with him? Here is an example:

"I've read your profile and...

... I'm very interested in your work field and I would like to be part of your network and follow your updates".

... I'm looking to connect with people with the same concerns as me".

... I find your publications and your work very interesting and I would be pleased if we could connect".

You are being polite, and open to a dialogue. Not a spammer (there are spammers in this network too)

Second Rule: LinkedIn is for your personal branding, not for your company branding (if you are working for one). You can connect with people you've met doing business and that you've worked with, of course. But don't try to find new contacts just to sell them something, or even worse, to sell them something from your company. You are burning bridges. Hank Blanks (a LinkedIn Personal Branding Influencer) says: *"the only truth that matters is not where you work but your character and your personal brand, because that can't be fired, that can't be reduced.*

That can only grow".

Tips
- Your profile must be always updated.
- Post professional content and news.
- Find interest groups.
- If you are looking for a job, follow and join all employment groups you can find.
- Talk to your contacts, comment on their best posts and participate in the dialogue.
- Think about the idiom first before you create your default profile. It cannot be changed. All other profiles you add in other languages will be secondary. Have profiles in at least two languages: English and your native one.

GOOGLE PLUS

You are probably thinking... what about Google+? *Isn't it a top social network?*

Truth is I don't want to waste a single moment on this question, so I will summarize my answer:

Google+ is rubbish.

There is nothing you can do on this social network you cannot do using Twitter, Facebook or LinkedIn. It's the way it is. Google+ is like the school bully, always waiting to get your lunch money. If you use Android or Gmail, you will see that around every corner there is a suggestion to create your Google plus profile... And most of the time, you will already have one without knowing it...

And that is because it's rubbish. It's like the arrogant person everyone has in their company or at school that believes they are better than you just because they are rich and because their father is a rock star.

The only way Google+ could be remotely interesting is for SEO. It's his father's son. Every post you publish on this social network is going to have a better SEO than any other. So, be smart; act like the child that gets paid by the other child's father to go to the birthday party. Go, eat cake and come back home with your real friends.

Share everything you create for other networks on Google+. That's all the use this network can offer you.

9 THE PROFESSIONAL BLOG

The blog is the perfect tool to boost our personal branding image. It's almost like having a website. It's a place of our own, where we can develop our personal brand.

Of course, there are many types of blogs: personal, anonymous, with various authors, one author, blogs that feed from other blogs, and also, the kind we are going to take special notice of, **the professional one.**

We can use the blog to show (professionally) what we know. Think about it. Your professional career and expertise can be written in a couple of pages. You can indicate all of this in a resume, but how can you prove it's true? How can you convince someone that has never met you, worked with you, or even heard about you that you do what you claim to do?

The moment you can do that, you will start building up your personal brand!

The best way to show and convince is using a blog: a

professional one.

Imagine you say you can clear custom requirements for shipments from foreign countries. That is a hell of a skill if you are an economic agent looking for customers or if you are searching for a job in logistics. That skill is only one line in a resume or just a couple of words in a business card. However, what if you use your blog to publish a guide about how to do the custom clearance? What if you show step by step how to do it?

Then why they should hire me?

Look at the big picture. You are never going to give all details on how to do it. Or maybe you will. It doesn't matter. If you give all the details on a complicated and complex process, many people are going to use the guide to do the process by themselves instead hiring you. But you will start to become a very valued expert. You are investing in yourself. At the beginning you have to compromise your best work. You are trying to be different, right? It's a way to gain status, to become a reference.

Publishing articles, guides, manuals, research works or just advice is a perfect way to promote ourselves in a very convincing way. We are not showing off or being pretentious. We are sharing what we know with others, collaborating and creating relationships.

For those of you that lack professional experience, (you've recently finished university or you've changed your specialty) starting a blog is your entrance to the game. Little by little you can start talking about what you are a specialized in.

- *What is your specialized field?*
- *Graphic designer*

- *Can you tell me about your previous experience:*

A: (without blog): *I've been unemployed the last 2 years / I have just finished my studies and I'm looking for my first opportunity.*

B: (with blog): *In the last 2 years I've been working for myself, trying to create a job rather than look for one. You can check out some of my work on my website / Even though I've finished my studies this year, it's been a couple of years since I started to share professional content and work for myself every time I had an opportunity. You can check out part of my work...*

When you talk about certain topics, you also are forced to get better. You start looking at the sources, selecting the best. You answer questions (so you begin to lose your fear of dialoguing). As time goes by, you feel more confident and you learn more about your field and yourself.

There are many ways and tools to create a blog. The most powerful and well known are: Wordpress, Blogger (Google) and BlogSpot (Hispavista). All of them are very easy to manage. They all come with a configuration wizard or an assistant, templates, themes, structures and widgets. You don't need to be a web expert to get it running **in a jiffy**. You can insert different types of files: video, text, pictures, audio tracks, presentations, datasheets, databases and many others. So, once again, it's perfect for sharing content.

As with any other tool, a professional blog has a series of rules you need to know to use it effectively and efficiently.

Rules:

Be patient: A professional blog is like a marathon. It's a long-distance race with a series of hurdles that have to be cleared along the way. Do not expect results in a couple of months. At the beginning you will have just a few visitors.

Relevancy: You need to write articles. It's not about the quantity, but the quality. The content must be interesting, relevant useful and it's what your visitors are looking for.

Personal Opinions: You should never use your professional blog for personal opinions about politics, religions or any other topic not related to professional issues. For these kinds of opinions, you can create another blog: a personal one. The personal opinions you can share in a professional blog are related to project or job experiences. How did they make you feel, how you solved the problems, etc. These are good. They humanize you and will make people empathize with you.

Update: Recheck topics you talked about and update them if necessary. Maybe some laws have changed the context or there has been a new development.

Publications: You need to post in a recurrent way, maybe monthly, weekly, twice a month... Whatever suits you. But be constant. For a blog, a minimum of five time every two months.

Comment moderation: Comments are good; don't filter them. They are either good or bad opinions. It will give you credibility. However, review comments before they are published. This is a measure to avoid SPAM, or for blogging, JAM. (This is a comment that seems legitimate, but it has a link to an external website where you usually are asked to buy Viagra or watch porn).

Biography: Add a page or a widget inside the blog where people can click and get to know the author. People like to know who is behind the entries. Add your other social links too.

Be a team player: Look for other blogs like yours. Follow and read people's blogs that have your same concerns. Connect with them, collaborate and look for collaboration. **Networking**.

Followers: Eventually, you will get followers. They will subscribe to your blog to get updates when a new entry comes out. Please, do not use these email addresses or any other details commercially. Don't sell that information. Don't be a spammer.

Never publish sensitive information regarding the current company you are working for. It's very irresponsible. For some articles, you may have to ask permission if there is a possible conflict of interest.

Types of blogs:

Researcher blog: The entries have a long extension. You can find guides, manuals and research jobs. This blog is focused on dissemination. Each entry has a lot of work behind it and they are high-value. With this blog, you won't have many visitors, but they will be the most faithful followers. This is also called having "repeat visitors". This is a metric that measures the number of users that return to your website after a first visit to it. To keep it updated, it just requires one publication per month.

Journalist blog: This kind of blog is very useful when you publish *In-Depth Reviews or News*. You collect different sources and combine them to give the reader a bigger version of the story. When a reader is interested in an issue, they look everywhere for new information about it. The more the merrier. So you have to give it to them. You have to do the searching job and cover as many aspects as possible of that topic. The hard work is searching for and organizing all the content you find, and quoting all the sources. Although, there is also a certain difficulty in writing and giving form to the entry. You can come back in the future to update it, or create a series of publications (part 1, part 2…). The periodicity becomes shorter: twice or three times a month.

Tips blog: Use this kind of blog to share quick content. Normally, the entries are short. They describe a very specific topic in a very practical way. It's the typical, "10 rules about…", "5 things you should/shouldn't…", "facts about…" etc. They are very fast and easy to read. Of course, it's the blog with the most visitors and shares. You need to post at least once a week, and you need to be very careful about what you write, too. It's imperative that you can backup what you write with scientific facts. It's a good blog for people who already have a strong personal brand; they are well positioned and respected. The "returning visitors" stat is low, although you have a very high amount of visitors.

Mixed blog: Obviously, a professional blog doesn't need to fit in one of the above categories. You can write articles of each type and combine them depending on the topic and what you want to share.

Type	Length of each entry	Publication Periodicity	Number of Visitors	Impact and relevancy
Researcher	Long	Once a month	Low but huge number of repeat visitors	Maximum – The content is high value. The audience is concentrated
Journalist	Medium or Long	Twice a month	Medium – High	High – Content is a source of sources. Good value. Audience starts to be dispersed
Tips	Short	Each week	Huge, but low number of repeat visitors	Low – Many people do the same thing. Difficult to differentiate from others.

10 IMPACT

One of the main problems we have to resolve is "at what time should I post to maximize the impact?" Maximizing the impact is not only visibility, but also, achieving a high click count.

Nothing is more effective than experience. Eventually you will know when your followers are more active.

However, there is a regular behavior in each social network. Depending on the nature of the network, people will connect, comment and share at certain time. Almost all people inside that platform have that common behavior. So you can take advantage of it, and publish when it's supposed to have more impact.

Bitly (a link shortener), published a study about when to post. It's very accurate, so let's analyze it for Twitter and Facebook.

Twitter
For Twitter, posting in the afternoon earlier in the week

is your best option (1-3pm Monday through Thursday). Posting after 8pm should be avoided. Specifically, don't bother posting after 3pm on a Friday. Twitter doesn't work on weekends.

The peak traffic times for Twitter are 9am through 3pm, Monday through Thursday. Posting on Twitter when there are many people clicking does help raise the average number of clicks, but it in no way guarantees an optimal amount of attention, since there is more competition for any individual's attention. An optimal strategy must weigh the number of people paying attention against the number of other posts vying for that attention.

Facebook
Between 1pm and 4pm you will have your best chance to achieve the highest average click through. The peak time of the week is on Wednesday at 3pm. Links posted after 8pm and before 8am will have more difficulty achieving high amounts of attention. As with Twitter, avoid posting on the weekends.

Conclusion
Each social network has its own culture and behavior patterns. By understanding the simple characteristics of each social network, you can publish your content at exactly the right time for it to reach the maximum number of people.

11   YOUR PROFILE OF ONLINE PROFILES

You are now in 4 or 5 social networks. You have your own blog and you are starting to share content across Internet.

What's coming next?
You need to create your own website.

But for some reason, you don't want to (or you can't). It's very simple to create a website in html or with Wordpress, but it's understandable that at the beginning, it can be a bit scary.

PERSONAL RECOMMENDATION FROM
THE OGRE:

My recommendation for you is to buy a template in html5, a responsive one. You can find it in some platforms like themefores. It will cost you around $15. Hosting service, with email accounts can be about $30 per year. That is all. It will take some time and a lot of effort, but it will be worth it.

Anyway, this book **isn't about how hard it can be,** but **how easy it can be**. So, how can you group all your public profiles into one? Are there any services? Free?
The solution is a profile of online profiles.

There are several services that can provide the solution you need. Also, they have the added value of positioning your profiles. There are several. I'm going to show you three of them and I will explain their pros and cons.

ABOUT.ME

This is a very simple and elegant solution. The site offers registered users a simple platform from which to link multiple online identities, relevant external sites, and popular social networking websites such as Facebook, Flickr, Google+, LinkedIn, Twitter, Tumblr, and YouTube. It is characterized by its one-page user profiles, each with a large, often-artistic background image and abbreviated biography.

It's ideal for a short description about yourself and your concerns. At first sight, the visitor will see all your online profiles and will be able to connect with them. SEO is magnificent, and it will probably be the second reference you will find on the internet when you Google your name (after LinkedIn).

It also gives you the opportunity of creating a custom button. The button "Hire me" is very interesting. By clicking on it, it will open a second page with your professional resume (taken from LinkedIn).

It's a free platform. There is, however, a premium version, where you can use a custom domain (yourname.me) instead of about.me/yourname. It also removes the about.me branding. Is it worth it? Well, the thing is, the free version is already pretty good.

It's very popular in the US, and it's the perfect complement for Twitter (use about.me for the short profile description of your twitter account).

STRIKINGLY.COM

Strikingly is a website builder. Possibly the best you can find. It uses a modern scroll down theme and is responsive. It works perfectly on mobile devices. You can customize it right away in the browser (you don't need any knowledge of html at all).

You can create new sections, add pictures, videos, etc. You can create your own website in minutes with a professional look. And it's free.

It only has one con: the theme itself. Scroll down is starting to be mainstream, and I don't want you to think I'm a stupid hipster. The point is everyone is using the same type of theme. There is nothing you can do to make it different.

They all look the same!

Don't get me wrong, if you don't have your own website, this one is very good and you should try it.

There is also a premium version, where you can use your own domain. It costs 96 bucks, and that's a lot for having your custom domain, but it will give you a custom email address too. It's up to you, but modifying an html5 theme is not that hard, and buying your own domain and hosting is much cheaper and will provide you more control.

SEO is not very good, but as we said before, it's better than nothing.

4ORMAT.COM

4ormat is a professional online portfolio with many themes to choose from. All of them are responsive. Like before with Strikingly, you can create different sections. You can create a section to talk about your work, your social profiles, your skills, etc. The biggest difference is the customization. It's very good, and you can really make the difference.

One big con. 4ormat is not for everyone. It targets **creative people** that have a portfolio. That portfolio can be pictures, designs, or any other **product.** I say product because if what you offer is a service, it's not the best platform to use.

SEO is very good, as good as about.me. And of course, it also has a premium service. But it's not that expensive. It's $70 per year. 4ormat will grant you a custom domain, a subdomain, blog service and social integration.

12   HOOTSUITE

At this point, you are ready to start connecting, communicating and sharing content with people. You have profiles in LinkedIn, Twitter, Facebook, a blog and a personal website.

How can I manage all of that? How can I be up to date? How can I be aware of everything that happens to my audience?

You knew that boosting your personal brand could be very hard, and you were ready to dedicate some time to being in the loop, but you are realizing it's impossible. It looks like you need many hours to check everything so nothing slips through the cracks. **You cannot be online 24/7.**
You cannot expect to be listened to if you don't do it. You want people to read your work, share your content, contact, reply and start conversations. The problem is you

need to do the same. And it takes time.

Question: Controlling everything requires a lot of time, and I don't have it. Is there any tool I can use?
Answer: Yes. It's called a **Social Media Management System (SMMS).**

And the best, by far, is **Hootsuite** (http://hootsuite.com/). Hootsuite is a social media management system for brand management. The system's user interface takes the form of a dashboard, and supports social network integrations for Twitter, Facebook, LinkedIn, Google+, Foursquare, MySpace and Wordpress. Additionally, you can install apps (called integrations) available on its app directory (like Instagram, Reddit, Blogger or YouTube).
It's an online dashboard (so you can access it everywhere and from any device) where you can see all your online profiles at once.

And it gets better.

If you already have a Twitter account, you can use it to sign in. The free version of the platform allows you to add **five different profiles to the dashboard. That's** more than enough for a Personal Branding Strategy.
You can organize the dashboard by desktops, and in each one, add as many columns as you want. You choose what each column displays. For example, for Twitter: mentions, direct messages, last tweets or status of your network, marked as favorites, shared, retweets or lists. You are breaking down the notification tool of each network into columns.
You can schedule your publications. This is a huge

relief. If you have a job, you cannot be publishing in social networks during your work time. Also, as we saw before, there are certain hours that are better than others for posting content (higher impact). With this tool, you can set the time, the day, the format and the social networks where you want your content to be posted.

Twitter Lists. When you create a list in Twitter, it can be added as a column into your dashboard. So you can visualize what's going on in the blink of an eye. This is, probably, the most powerful tool you have to create engagement with your followers.

Notifications. You can have all your notifications in one place.

It's all about **control and order**. Being up to date is hard. Without a SMMS, you would have to check everything network by network. With a SMMS, you have all the information in one place, ordered according to your preferences and, of course, in realtime.

Create a desktop with all the lists we talked about in the Twitter chapter.

Create a search column for each network with key terms (words) about the topic you want to be updated.

13 OTHER NETWORKS

There are many other social networks that could be very interesting for us. Some of them are focused in one sector or field (foreign trade, design, microblogging, news about social media, etc.) and other are specific for a certain language or country. You are the only one that decides if they can help you or not (Not all of them are listed here, but all those listed are indeed good networks):

Bebo (www.bebo.com): Bebo is a social networking website launched in 2005. The site is now mobile only, with 3 new apps launched under the BEBO brand. It was sold in 2008 and bought back in 2013. It was very popular in the UK and Ireland.

Digg (www.digg.com): Digg is a news aggregator with an editorially driven front page, aiming to select stories specifically for the internet audience, such as science, trending political issues, and <u>viral</u> Internet issues. It was launched in its current form on July 31, 2012, with support for sharing content to other social platforms such as Twitter and Facebook.

Domestika (http://www.domestika.org): Domestika is the largest and most influential Spanish-speaking community for creative professionals. In Domestika creative professionals can share their projects, contribute and learn in forums, connect with other designers, and find employment.

Draugiem.lv (www.draugiem.lv/): Draugiem is a social networking website launched in 2004. It is the largest social networking website in Latvia with approx. 2.6 million registered users

Flickr (www.flickr.com/): Flickr is an image hosting and video hosting website acquired by Yahoo. In addition to being a popular website for users to share and embed personal photographs, and effectively an online community, the service is widely used by photo researchers and by bloggers to host images that they embed in blogs and social media.

Foursquare (www.foursquare.com): Foursquare is a location-based social networking website for mobile devices, such as smartphones. Users "check in" at venues using a mobile website, text messaging or a device-specific application by selecting from a list of venues that the application locates nearby.

Google+ (https://plus.google.com/): Google Plus is the social network operated by Google. It's a mix of Twitter and Facebook, but way worse. The only good thing is the SEO of your profile on Google.

Instagram (http://instagram.com/): Instagram is an online mobile photo-sharing, video-sharing and social networking service that enables its users to take pictures and videos, apply digital filters to them, and share them on social networks. A distinctive feature is that it confines photos to a square shape.

La Cancillería (www.lacancilleria.com): La Cancilleria is a Spanish-speaking community for international trade professionals.

Mashable (www.mashable.com): Mashable is a British-American news website, technology and social media blog. The website's primary focus is social media news, but it also covers news and developments in mobile, entertainment, online video, business, web development, technology, memes and gadgets.

Medium (https://medium.com/): Medium is the blog complement of twitter. This social network allows you to tell stories without the 140 character limitation. The good thing about Medium is that you can log in with your Google account and just write a post. You won't need to worry about format, themes, configuration, etc. Write and post.

Menéame (http://meneame.net/): Menéame is a Spanish social news website based in community participation, made for users to discover and share content from anywhere on the internet, by submitting links and stories and voting and commenting on submitted links and stories. Its model is based on Digg and it combines Social bookmarking, blogging and Web syndication with a publication system without editors.

Mixi (https://mixi.jp/): Mixi is an online Japanese social networking service.

Nexopia (www.nexopia.com): Nexopia is a Canadian social networking website for people aged 13 and up. Users are able to create and design their own profiles, friends list, blogs, galleries, articles, and forums. It has an internal personal messaging system and public users comment on profiles, blogs or through threads and posts on the forums.

Odnoklassniki (http://odnoklassniki.ru/): Odnoklassniki (Одноклассники) is a social network service for classmates and old friends. It is popular in Russia and former Soviet Republics. The site claims that it has more than 200 million registered users and 45 million daily unique visitors.

Orkut (http://orkut.com/): Orkut is a social networking website owned and operated by Google for India and Brazil. The service is designed to help users meet new and old friends and maintain existing relationships.

Pinterest (www.pinterest.com): Pinterest is a visual discovery tool that people use to collect ideas for their different projects and interests. People create and share collections (called "boards") of visual bookmarks (called "Pins") that they use to do things like plan trips and projects, organize events or save articles and recipes. Globally, the site is most popular with women (86% in

2012).

Reddit (http://www.reddit.com/): Reddit is an entertainment, social networking service and news website where registered community members can submit content, such as text posts or direct links. Only registered users can then vote submissions "thumbs up" or "down" to organize the posts and determine their position on the site's pages. Content entries are organized by areas of interest called "subreddits".

Slideshare (www.slideshare.net): SlideShare is a Web 2.0 based slide hosting service. Users can upload files privately or publicly in the following file formats: PowerPoint, PDF, Keynote or OpenDocument presentations

Smarterer (http://smarterer.com/): Smarterer is an online skills tests platform. According to them: "Since 2010, hundreds of thousands of Smarterer users have taken over 2 million skills tests, answering over 29 million questions to prove their skills."

The Renren Network (http://renren.com/): Also known as the Xiaonei Network, it is a Chinese social networking service. It has been called the Facebook of China, popular amongst college students.

Tuenti (www.tuenti.es): Tuenti is a Spain-based, social networking service. It's a copy of Facebook that's very popular with teenagers. Since 2012 it has been growing globally.

Tumblr (https://tumblr.com/): Tumblr is a

microblogging platform and social networking website. The service allows users to post multimedia and other content to a short-form blog. Users can follow other users' blogs, as well as make their blogs private

Vimeo (www.vimeo.com/): Vimeo is a video-sharing website on which users can upload, share and view videos. It's very similar to YouTube

Vine (https://vine.co/): Vine is a mobile app owned by Twitter that enables its users to create and post short looping video clips. Video clips created with Vine have a maximum clip length of six seconds and can be shared to Vine's social network, or to other services such as Twitter and Facebook

VK (https://vk.com/): VK (Vkontakte) is the second largest social network service in Europe after Facebook. It is available in several languages, but particularly popular among Russian-speaking users around the world.

Weibo (http://weibo.com/): Weibo is the Chinese word for "microblog". It refers to mini-blogging services in China, including social chat sites and platform sharing.

Xing: (www.xing.com): It's is a social software platform for enabling a small-world network for professionals.

YouTube (www.YouTube.com): YouTube is a video-sharing website owned by Google since late 2006, on which users can upload, view and share videos. The user can create a channel and playlist. Videos can be shared with other social networks.

14 STYLE GUIDE WHEN SHARING

Creating content is **very** difficult. I'm not talking about writing content only, but pictures, infography, guides, slides, compositions, sounds, etc.

Part of being social is sharing content from others. So it's utterly important to follow some rules when sharing from a third party. Do it well and you will create a win-win situation.

1. BE SURE INFORMATION CAN BE SHARED

This is very useful when sharing content from friends. Ask them before sharing: "Can I share your content?" Maybe it's a picture, a phrase or an opinion they only want to share with friends, not with the general public.

2. NAME THE AUTHOR AND THE SOURCE

Always be clear with your audience and tell them where you got that information/post/picture... etc.

The sources matter... A good source is **updated, relevant and reliable.** The better sources you get, the better the information you give.

3. USE SHARING BUTTONS.

Use the share button when you copy an image (or download it to load it after), even if the image has the logo and the website. The reason is simple: SEO is based on links. The more links an author gets to their content, the more relevant it becomes and the better position it has (SEO). When you copy and paste into your own post, you are killing the link to the author, and stealing his positionation. So please, use share buttons. It's what Google does care about! You share the information; the author gets a better SEO! It's a win-win! If you don't do it, you improve the SEO of the picture but not the author. That means, people will find the picture from your website, not from the author's website. What you have done is steal their visitors! Not good at all!

4. LINK TO THE ORIGINAL PUBLICATION.

If what you want to share is a part of a whole publication, or that publication does not have sharing buttons (but you have permission from the author to publish it), you can provide a link to the original publication. It's a web reference and will help the author to get a better rank.

5. DON'T SHARE IF YOU CAN CAUSE ECONOMIC HARM.

Sometimes, an author can have an agreement with a company to publish only on his website. If that content gets in your lap, please, don't share it; tell the author (if possible) where you found it. Be responsible.

Style Guide *on*

Sharing Third Party Content

Remember these 5 simple rules next time you share content from someone else.
Please, creating content is very difficult, and authors deserve the credit

Be sure the information can be shared

Name the author and the source

Use the sharing buttons wherever possible

If you can't, give a link to the original publication

If you can cause economic harm, don't share

15 RECAP OF THE TOP THREE SOCIAL NETWORKS AND THE BLOG

Facebook	
Use a private account and control what you want to be public (articles, statuses, likes, educational info, etc.) If it's a fan page, it should be public.	**Privacy**
Pictures, news, links to articles and videos	**What to share?**
Lunch time. Users are also active during their afternoon breaks	**When?**

Twitter	
Public Basic control of what we want to publish	**Privacy**
Accurate information (use the hashtags), pictures and links to other relevant content. Create lists and check each one to answer and comment on your contacts' tweets.	**What to share?**
In the morning. You can repeat the tweet in different languages and at different times (i.e. a tweet in Spanish for Spain and 8 hours later in English for US and Canada)	**When?**

LinkedIn	
Public. Make your profile multi-language.	Privacy
News regarding the sector where you work or the one you are interested in. Participate in debates and join groups of your preferences (where your audience is). Be careful, do not share sensible information from former companies (or from a current one).	What to share?
Same as twitter.	When?

Blog/Website	
Public with comment control. You will need to approve them to be published.	**Privacy**
Everything you want, but without size restrictions. Opinions, guides, manuals, research, etc.	**What to share?**
At least, once a month.	**When?**

16 CHECKLIST – ROADMAP

- Do a self-critical analysis or a reflection about your current personal branding status.

- Set ambitious but realistic targets over the medium- and long- term.

- Prepare all prior documentation (public photo, contact info and an expert resume).

- Create your hint.

- Create an account in the main professional networks: LinkedIn and Xing (keep them updated).

- Create an account in Twitter and associate it with your

other profiles.

- Choose your own Hashtag.

- Manage your Facebook privacy options: total or partial (according to your needs).

- Search networks where you can find people or groups of your interest. Inside each network, check the groups related to your professional field and follow/get in contact with people with your same concerns.

- Create a blog and publish your works, studies, guides and books. It's a very good way of showing your expertise.

- Once you master the main social networks, keep searching for more specific ones adapted to your profile.

- Publish or post relevant information periodically (remember it's not a matter of quantity, but quality).

- Create networking. Participate in discussions, share your ideas, listen the others ideas. Communicate with others in a positive way.

- Be a leader by your deeds, not only by your words.

- Keep the good mood. Don't participate in discussions only to criticize. Get yourself noticed and share your work.

- Never insult. Never disrespect others.

- Be assertive.

- Set mid- to long-term goals.

- Evaluate your progress and adapt your actions and intensity in order to achieve your goals.

- Enjoy the process and learn. The world is full of wonderful things we can only get to know if we are "plugged in".

17 ONE LAST BE AWARE OF THE OGRE

You have to work on your personal branding periodically. It's very important to keep an optimistic attitude and use the tools we have seen responsibly and consistently. The most important thing is to maintain a good mood. Don't be a "troll"; don't be one of those that only engages in long polemics without creating real content and value. In the same way, don't let people put you on the edge, and don't take it personal. People are way different on the internet than in their real life.

Remember, personal branding is a "voluntary job", but still, it's a job. Try to compartmentalize it from your personal life. The same way it's not good take work home, you shouldn't take home to work.

I wish you the best of luck. I hope this book has helped

you (or will), and that if it hasn't, at least you had a good time.

Trust yourself, plan your present and design your future.

ABOUT THE AUTHOR

MANUEL VERA is specialized in foreign trade and social marketing. He was born in 1984 in Cordoba, Spain. He holds a degree in Business Administration from the University of Seville, a Masters in International Business Operations by the Chamber of Commerce and another in International Trade by the EOI. He has worked as a logistics manager for the Alter Group, as a consultant for the Commercial Office of the Embassy of Spain in London, and now as International Manager for a Spanish company. He is the founder of FT20, an online encyclopedia of foreign trade with over 70 articles, guides and manuals on international procedures. He is the author of other books like "International Sale Price" (2014), "Selling the moto" (2014), "Step by Step Guide Incoterms 2010" (2013) or "International Payment Methods" (2013).

www.ingramcontent.com/pod-product-compliance
Lightning Source LLC
Chambersburg PA
CBHW030902180526
45163CB00004B/1674